Before me, behind me,
always beside me
No shadow, no valley,
where You won't find me
I am not afraid at all

Bad dogs barking loud
Bad ghosts in a cloud
I am not afraid at all

Mean old Mother Goose
Lions on the Loose
I am not afraid at all

Dragons breathing flame
On my counterpane
I am not afraid at all

I go boo
Make them shoo
I make fun
Way they run
I won't cry
So they fly
I just smile
They go wild
I am not afraid at all

When I stand before the
power of hell
and death is at my side
I am not afraid at all

When I walk amid the burning flames

I will not be harmed

I am not afraid at all

Panthers in the park
Strangers in the dark
No, I am not afraid at all

When I walk through the waters,
I won't be overcome
I am not afraid at all

When I go through the rivers,
I will not be drowned
I'm not afraid at all

Made in the USA
Columbia, SC
04 February 2020

87483443R00015